Motherhood

1000 TALES
what's your story?

Celebrate the maternal experience in all its diversity.

First Published in 2017.
Copyright 1000 Tales Co-op Ltd.
All rights reserved.
This book or any portion thereof may not be reproduced,
stored in or introduced in a retrieval system, or transmitted,
in any form or by any means without the express written
permission of 1000 Tales Co-op Ltd except for the use of
brief quotations in a book review.

ISBN-13: 978-0-6481964-1-9

General enquiries
info@1000tales.org.au
(+61) 481 571 595

Shop
www.1000tales.org.au/shop

Contributors

Alaia Saheb

Ameera Karimshah

Anna Vassadis

Gayathiri Ganthithasan

Gurlovleen Kaur Sehmbi

Hayley Dry

Helén Haukedal

Imaani O'Reilly

Jessica Edwards

Jessica Parles Svendsen

Juliet Green

Lajla Darvill

Liyana Saheb

Nazrana Shbeb

Nazmeera O'Reilly

Shamina Khanum

Sharon Govender

Tahira Peer

Tanja Fitisemanu

Editorial

Ameera Karimshah

Cover Art

Jessica Edwards

Graphic Design

Shabnaaz Sheik Ahmed

About this book

The Motherhood Project aims to celebrate the maternal experience in all its diversity. The project came about in recognition of the growing need to re-establish the 'village' for the modern world. We hope that by showcasing the experiences of motherhood we can provide a small insight into the shared spaces that mothers occupy. We also hope that in reading this book you will recognize elements of your experience in some stories and appreciate the diversity of others. Through this collection we aim to inspire a sense of togetherness among women and their communities.

Who we are

1000 tales is a cooperative that aims to provide an outlet for storytelling that reflects the lived experiences of culturally and linguistically diverse people. 1000 tales was formed to create an ecosystem in which stories that are not usually told can be nurtured. We hope to create a platform by which people can share these stories through beautiful books, magazines and other publications that honour the energy, memory and ceremony of their particular experience. Please show your support and help us to give voice to more stories that matter. 1000 tales is a not for profit and all proceeds from the sale of this book will be used to fund further projects.

A Letter To My Baby Boy

To my dear son,

It's been a short time since I had the pleasure of meeting you. Since that wonderful day, life has changed tremendously. My days are now filled with the numerous tasks associated with caring for you. There's very little time for myself, I'm always tired, and it's certainly not all about me anymore. It didn't take long to realise that life will never be the same. But I'm okay with it. In fact, I wouldn't have it any other way. I wholeheartedly accept my new role because you're so very worth it. Your presence is magical. I try to take it all in, to savour every day. I especially revel in the tender, quiet times between us. Peering down at you as you feed, I hope to forever capture the moment in my mind. To always remember your sweet scent, the sound of your soft steady breathing, the warmth created between us by holding you close, the way you slowly drift into a peaceful slumber. I treasure the way you clutch my hand, as if I'm your everything. Watching you sleep, I'm in awe of how quickly you're growing and developing. Your feet now dangle to the side of my lap when it was only a few weeks ago that they nestled into my side. Such a strong reminder of how our time together is so precious.

I often think about how much I've gained since you came into this world. I may have given you the gift of life, but what you've bestowed upon me with your arrival is far greater. You see, I feel as if I've become selfless, much more compassionate, caring and patient. I now possess a great strength and power. You have taught me so many things in such a short time. To appreciate life and every moment I'm able to spend living. To take a breath, slow down, and enjoy the little things. To focus on me, especially my own happiness and wellbeing. But best of all, you have taught me how to be a mother. There is no greater gift. It's an honour to be your mama and a responsibility I take on with utmost pride, enthusiasm and dedication. Thank you my sweetheart, you have given me so much.

I have so many hopes and dreams for you. Most importantly, I hope that life brings you much happiness and love. I want to teach you to have a heart for others, to be kinds, generous and giving. I want to motivate you to find your passion, and to be brave enough to pursue whatever it is that makes you happy. I want to encourage you to voice your thoughts, feelings and opinions. I promise to listen to you so that you will always feel like you are heard. I won't always give you what you want, but I'll strive to make sure that you always have what you need. I will remind you that life is tough and can be cruel at times. In doing so, I hope to ensure that you possess the strength to overcome any struggles and hardships, to be resilient and to always remain optimistic. To have great courage and a fighting spirit.

I'm proud of you and love you very much.

Your mama.

Letter & Photography by Anna Vassadis

"Mummy sells people's money. Daddy catches all the badies. He is a policeman. Baby Aleena is just with Mummy and Daddy" — Imaani

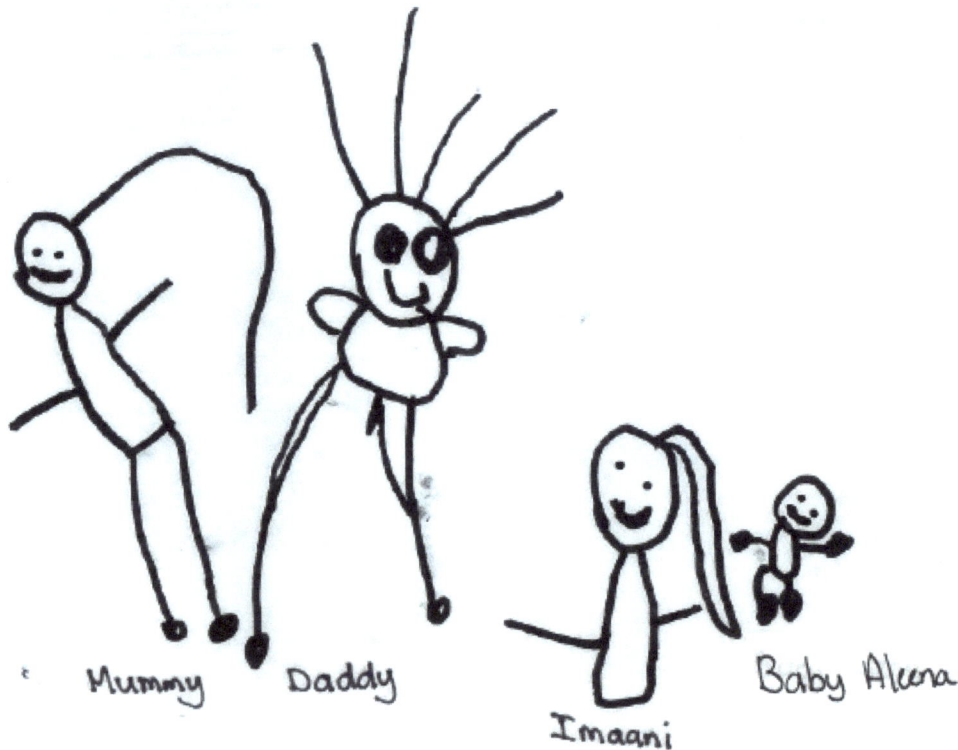

Imaani drew this picture at kindergarten, her teacher asked her to draw a picture of her family and to provide her understanding of her parents roles in their respective jobs. I am a little sentimental when it comes to the artwork she has created, and as such have kept every piece since she started childcare. This particular piece is the first in which she has drawn people. It also includes her little sister who was born a month after the picture was drawn which makes it even more special.

I do need to clarify, that I do not sell people's money...I work in a bank.

Mummy   Daddy

Imaani

Baby Aleena

Story by Nazmeera O'Rielly
Artwork by Imaani O'Rielly

What I have learnt since becoming a mother is that we as adults limit ourselves too much and put ourselves into boxes of our own making and societies making, Kinnera has taught me to appreciate the small things in life and that only through failure we can succeed, she keeps trying to do new things every day, every minute, she never gives up and finds Joy in the smallest things.

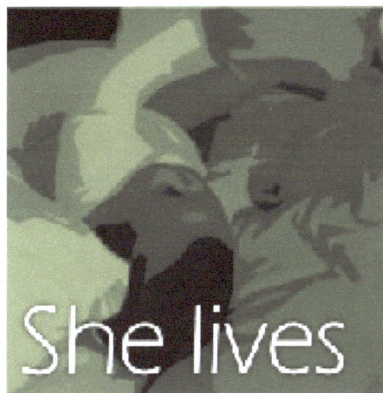

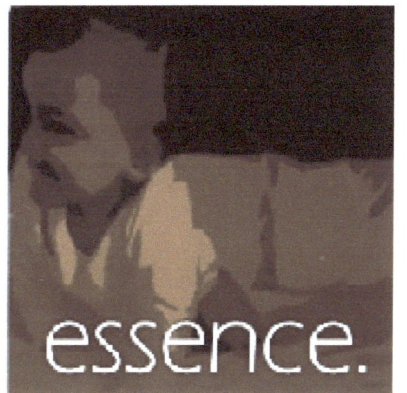

Story & Photography by Sharon Govender

Failure & Success

Joy

in her every breath

She lives life's essence.

Motherhood

தாய்மை

மகளாய் பிறந்தாள்
சகோதரியாக வளர்ந்தாள்
தோழியாக தோள் கொடுத்தாள்
காதலியாக மலர்ந்தாள்
மனைவியாக கரம் பிடித்தாள்
உருவானாள் பெண்ணாக.

சுமந்தாள் உயிரை கருவறையில்
மறு பிறப்பெடுத்தாள், தாயானாள்.
மறந்தாள் ஊண் உறக்கம்
தொலைத்தாள் தன் சுகம்.
அகமகிழ்ந்தாள் மழலையின் சிரிப்பில்.
தன்னை மறந்தாள் சேயின் தழுவலில்.

பாசத்தையும் பண்பையும் கொடுத்தாள்.
அன்பையும் அறிவையும் ஊட்டினாள்.
தைரியத்தையும் தெளிவையும் புகட்டினாள்.
நன்னடத்தையும் தன்னடக்கமும் கற்பித்தாள்.
மிளிர்ந்தாள் தாய்மையில்.
உயர்ந்தாள் தாயாய்.

கா. காயத்திரி.

Motherhood

Born as a daughter
As a sister, she grew
As a friend, was there to support
Flourished in love.
As a wife, held hands in marriage.
Emerged as a woman.

Carried a soul within her
Reborn as a mother.
Forgot her hunger, sleep and herself.
In her child's smile, she rejoiced
In her child's embrace, she lost herself

She lavished affection and character
Fed love and knowledge
She gave courage and clarity
She imbued good deeds and self-control
She glowed in motherhood
She bloomed as a mother.

Poem written in Tamil & English
Poem & Photography by Gayathiri Ganthithasan

ਮਾਂ ਦੇ ਦਿਲ ਦੇ ਅਹਿਸਾਸ

ਪੰਜ ਸਾਲ ਪਹਿਲਾਂ ਤੈਨੂੰ ਮੈਂ ਪਹਿਲੀ ਵਾਰ ਆਪਣੇ ਗਲ ਲਾਇਆ, ਤੇਰੀ ਮਾਸੂਮ ਮੁਸਕਾਨ ਦੇਖ ਕੇ ਮੇਰਾ ਦਿਲ ਭਰ ਆਇਆ। ਉਸ ਦਿਨ 2 ਅਪ੍ਰੈਲ 2013 ਨੂੰ ਸਾਡਾ ਸੰਸਾਰ ਬਦਲ ਗਿਆ, ਸਾਡੀ ਦੁਨੀਆ ਤੇਰੇ ਆਲੇ ਦੁਆਲੇ ਘੁੰਮਣ ਲਗ ਪਈ। ਅਗਮ-ਜਿਸਨੂੰ ਮੈਂ ਸੁਖਮਨੀ ਸਾਹਿਬ ਦੇ ਪੰਨਿਆਂ ਵਿਚੋਂ ਚੁਣਿਆ -ਬੇਅੰਤ ਨੂੰ ਦਰਸਾਉਂਦਾ ਹੈ। ਤੂੰ ਸੱਚ ਹੀ ਬਹੁਤ ਪਿਆਰ ਕਰਨ ਵਾਲਾ ਬੱਚਾ ਹੈ। ਤੇਰੇ ਦਿਲ ਵਿੱਚ ਬੇਅੰਤ ਹੀ ਹਮਦਰਦੀ ਤੇ ਦਇਆ ਭਰੀ ਹੈ ਜੋ ਸ਼ਾਇਦ ਹੀ ਮੈਂ ਕਿਸੇ ਵਿੱਚ ਦੇਖੀ ਹੈ।

ਇਹਨਾਂ ਪੰਜ ਸਾਲਾਂ ਵਿੱਚ ਤੇਰੀ ਸ਼ਖਸੀਅਤ ਵਿੱਚ ਬਹੁਤ ਬਦਲਾਵ ਆਇਆ ਹੈ। ਤੂੰ ਮਾਸੂਮ ਅਤੇ ਭੋਲੇ ਬੱਚੇ ਤੋਂ ਮੇਰੇ ਨੱਕ 'ਚ ਦਮ ਕਰਨ ਵਾਲਾ ਸ਼ਰਾਰਤੀ ਬੱਚਾ ਬਣ ਗਿਆ ਹੈ। ਮੈਨੂੰ ਅੱਜ ਵੀ ਉਹ ਦਿਨ ਯਾਦ ਹੈ ਜਦ ਮੈਂ ਤੈਨੂੰ ਪਹਿਲੀ ਵਾਰ ਰੁੜਦਾ ਦੇਖਿਆ ਸੀ, ਮੇਰੀ ਖੁਸ਼ੀ ਦਾ ਕੋਈ ਠਿਕਾਨਾ ਨਹੀਂ ਸੀ। ਤੇ ਹੁਣ ਤੈਨੂੰ ਇੱਕ ਪਲ ਚੈਨ ਲੈਣਾ ਵੀ ਮੰਜੂਰ ਨਹੀਂ ਹੈ। ਤੇਰੇ ਅਣਥੱਕ ਸਵਾਲ ਤੇ ਸਭ ਕੁਝ ਸਿੱਖਣ ਦੀ ਉਤਸੁਕਤਾ ਮੈਨੂੰ ਹੈਰਾਨ ਕਰ ਦਿੰਦੀ ਹੈ। ਪਰ ਇੱਕ ਚੀਜ਼ ਜੋ ਕਦੇ ਨਹੀਂ ਬਦਲੀ ,ਉਹ ਹੈ ਤੇਰੀ ਮਾਸੂਮ ਮੁਸਕਾਨ ਜੋ ਮੈਂ ਪਹਿਲੀ ਵਾਰ ਦੇਖੀ ਸੀ। ਕਾਸ਼ ਮੈਂ ਇਸ ਸਮੇਂ ਨੂੰ ਰੋਕ ਸਕਦੀ ਤਾਂ ਜੋ ਤੇਰੀ ਮਾਸੂਮੀਅਤ ਨੂੰ ਇਸ ਸੁਆਰਥੀ ਦੁਨੀਆ ਤੋਂ ਬਚਾ ਕੇ ਰੱਖ ਸਕਦੀ।

ਇਸ ਜਨਵਰੀ 2018 'ਚ ਤੂੰ ਸਕੂਲ ਸ਼ੁਰੂ ਕੀਤਾ। ਸਕੂਲ ਦੇ ਪਹਿਲੇ ਦਿਨ ਮੈ ਉਲਝਣ ਵਿੱਚ ਸੀ,ਮੇਰਾ ਦਿਲ ਭਰਿਆ ਤੇ ਅੱਖਾਂ ਨਮ ਸਨ। ਪਰ ਤੇਰੇ ਉਤਸ਼ਾਹ ਤੇ ਹੌਂਸਲੇ ਨੇ ਮੈਨੂੰ ਭਰੋਸਾ ਦਿੱਤਾ ਕਿ ਹੁਣ ਤੂੰ ਕੁਝ ਜ਼ਿੰਮੇਵਾਰ ਹੋ ਗਿਆ ਹੈ। ਇਸ ਗਲ ਤੇ ਮੈਨੂੰ ਬੁਰਾ ਵੀ ਲੱਗਿਆ ਕਿ ਹੁਣ ਤੈਨੂੰ ਮੇਰੀ ਜ਼ਰੂਰਤ ਨਹੀਂ ਹੈ ਪਰ ਹੌਸਲਾ ਵੀ ਹੋਇਆ ਕਿ ਤੂੰ ਹੁਣ ਸਮਝਦਾਰ ਹੋ ਰਿਹਾ ਹੈ। ਤੈਨੂੰ ਸਕੂਲ ਵਿੱਚ ਅੱਗੇ ਵਧਦਾ ਦੇਖ ਕੇ ਮੈਨੂੰ ਬਹੁਤ ਗਰਵ ਮਹਿਸੂਸ ਹੁੰਦਾ ਹੈ ਤੇ ਮੈਨੂੰ ਯਕੀਨ ਹੈ ਕਿ ਤੂੰ ਮੇਰੀ ਸਭ ਤੋਂ ਵੱਡੀ ਤਾਕਤ ਬਣੇਗਾ। ਤੇਰੀ ਹੋਂਦ ਨੇ ਮੈਨੂੰ ਵਿਸ਼ਵਾਸ ਦਿਲਵਾਇਆ ਹੈ ਕਿ ਪਿਆਰ ਕਿੰਨਾ ਅਸਾਧਾਰਨ ਹੁੰਦਾ ਹੈ।

ਰੱਬ ਤੈਨੂੰ ਹਮੇਸ਼ਾ ਚੜ੍ਹਦੀ ਕਲਾ 'ਚ ਰੱਖੇ , ਤੂੰ ਬਹੁਤ ਤਰੱਕੀ ਕਰੇਂ । ਤੇਰਾ ਦਿਲ ਹਮੇਸ਼ਾ ਪਿਆਰ ਨਾਲ ਭਰਿਆ ਰਹੇ ਤੇ ਰੱਬ ਤੈਨੂੰ ਸੁਮੱਤ ਬਖਸ਼ੇ।

ਬਹੁਤ ਬਹੁਤ ਪਿਆਰ

ਮਾਂ

It's been 5 years since I first held you, your smile snuggled right into my heart. On the 2nd April 2013, suddenly our universe shifted and you became our axis ....Our tiny little world – AGAM - which itself means unlimited. I have never seen such an inbuilt empathy and compassion in anyone. I am so grateful to God for such a wonderful gift.

You have changed a lot in 5 years. Your personality has turned out from the itsy bitsy snuggly sleepy bundle to a shrieky bumpy musketeer who climbs on me like I'm a jungle gym. You went from rolling, to crawling to walking and jumping to swimming and cycling!!!! . Your endless questions annoys the hell out of me (you got it from me-I know my mum says it's karma). One thing which never changed is your bright smile and unlimited cuteness which can make any heart melt. From little messy one to a keen helper, you are growing really fast which I wish I could slow down a bit. You are a beautiful human being who believes in so much love and affection that I can ignore the tantrums you throw here and there.

This year you joined the big school (as you say it). With a worried heart and teary eyes I stepped in the school, but you were so confident and super excited that I had to question myself. This made me realise that you are a big boy now, who doesn't want his mama for everything. I cried at the thought that you don't need me anymore but was happy to see you so grown up. I am so proud of you for the excellence you show in school and I am sure you will be my biggest strength.

You make me realize that my love is inexhaustible and I have promised myself to be there for you forever no matter what.

God bless you with lots of strength, good health, a caring heart and unending curiosity to learn. May you have good reasoning so you can differentiate between right and wrong in your life.

Love you always my sugar plum.

Mum xoxo.

Letter written in Punjabi & English
Letter & Photography by Gurlovleen Kaur Sehmbi

A Shining Star

My guide;
Beginning the next long journey
Nestled exactly where you need to be;
Underneath the last flower

Your father, born on a pearl
Raised by nature
Gifted only by the earth and the sea
And held by the brown hands that will also teach you
About both sides of your beautiful world

My gaze has shifted from what is behind us
From what is dark, like closed eyes
Opening to a backyard dappled with sunlight
by a dancing emerald curtain
And bird sounds in the warm air, like floral gossamer
Barefoot. Grounded
My gaze rests now upon a blooming dream

A shining star
My guide;
Herald me into fullness, my heart
From a crescent to a full moon
Where we place our hands
A warm glow behind the silhouette, a playful shadow you
can follow with your tiny fingers and toes

You are growing with the beat of my soul
A sound that will protect you
And love you
And learn from you
Until the day it slows and stops
Until I am reborn
To be once again by your side, because now I know
I am blessed

From a crescent to a full moon
Even more love for you, held by the infinite sky
Your ancestors, in their celestial body
The poya nights, the sunrise after
The falling water we love
And your sibling resting on the rainbow

Your story has been written up there
My guide;
You are the shining star

Artwork by Jessica Edwards
Poem by Heyley Dry

Moja najdraža kćeri,

Učinila si me majkom. Naučila si me strpljenju, naučila si me iskrenom, čistom, bezuvjetnom i nesebičnom ljubavlju.
Napunila si mi srce sa ljubavlju i srećom i sa svakim osmjehom, hihotom i svakom suzom, moja ljubav prema tebi je postajala sve snažnija.
Zauvijek ću se sjećati onih malih, samo naših trenutaka, kada si spavala u mojim rukama i ja sam gledala u tvoje prekrasne oči, savršen nos i usne.
Miris tvoje kože, mio zvuk tvog disanja.
Kako sam sretna što si me izabrala da budem tvoja majka.
Ti se nečeš sjećati tih trenutaka ali ja hoću. Uskoro ćeš biti prevelika da spavaš u mojim rukama ali ja ću uvijek čuvati te trenutke i sjećati se tog osjećaja potpunosti.

Moj najdraži sine,
Naučio si me da moje srce može narasti još veće. Pokazao si mi.
Trenutak kada su te stavili u moje ruke, kada je tvoja meka koža dodirnula moju, osjetila sam kako moje srce raste i puni se sa bezuvjetnom ljubavlju za tebe. U tome trenutku, samo smo ti i ja postojali na ovome svijetu, dok sam ti tiho šapnula 'Hvala ti što si me izabrao'.
Primjećujem kako ti se oči sjaje sa ljubavlju i divljenjem dok gledaš svoju veliku sestru i zaštitnički zagrljaji koje ti ona daje - moje srce je na miru. Osjećam spokoj. Znam, da bez obzira što se dogodi, vi ćete uvijek imati jedno drugo.

Moja najdraža djeco, naučili ste me kako voljeti bezuvjetno i poželjeti vam dati sve a ne tražiti isto zauzvrat. Dala sam vam svoje srce ispunjeno ljubavlju i obećanje da nikada neće biti sami na ovome velikome svijetu. Svaki osmijeh, svaki hihot, svaka suza. Tu sam uz vas i uvijek ću biti. Hvala vam što ste me učinili vašom mamom. Volim vas do mjeseca…i natrag.
Moja ljubav, moj život, moja duša, moja sreća. Moje sve.

My darling daughter,
You made me a mother. You taught me patience, you taught me true, pure, unconditional and unselfish love. You filled my heart with love and joy and with every smile, every giggle and every tear my love for you grew stronger.

I will forever cherish the little moments between just you and me, as you slept in my arms I gazed at your beautiful eyes, perfect nose and lips. The scent of your skin, the sweet sound of your breathing.
How lucky I am for you to have chosen me as your mother.
You will not remember those moments but I will. You will soon be too big to rest cuddled in my arms but I will always treasure those moments and remember the feeling of completeness.

My darling son,
You taught me that my heart can grow even more. You showed me.
The moment they put you in my arms, as your soft skin touched mine, I felt my heart growing bigger and fill with unconditional love for you. At that moment, it was only you and me in the world as I quietly whispered 'Thank you for choosing me'.

I notice your eyes sparkle with love and admiration as you look at your big sister and the protective hugs she gives you - my heart is at peace. I feel calm. I know, that no matter what happens, you will always have each other.

My darling children,
You taught me how to love unconditionally and made me want to give my all without asking for the same in return. I gave you my heart filled with love and a promise that you will never walk alone in this big world. Every smile, every giggle, every tear. I am here for you and always will be. Thank you for making me your mama. I love you right up to the moon…and back.

My love, my life, my soul, my happiness. My all.

Letter written in & English

Letter & Photography by Lajla Darvill

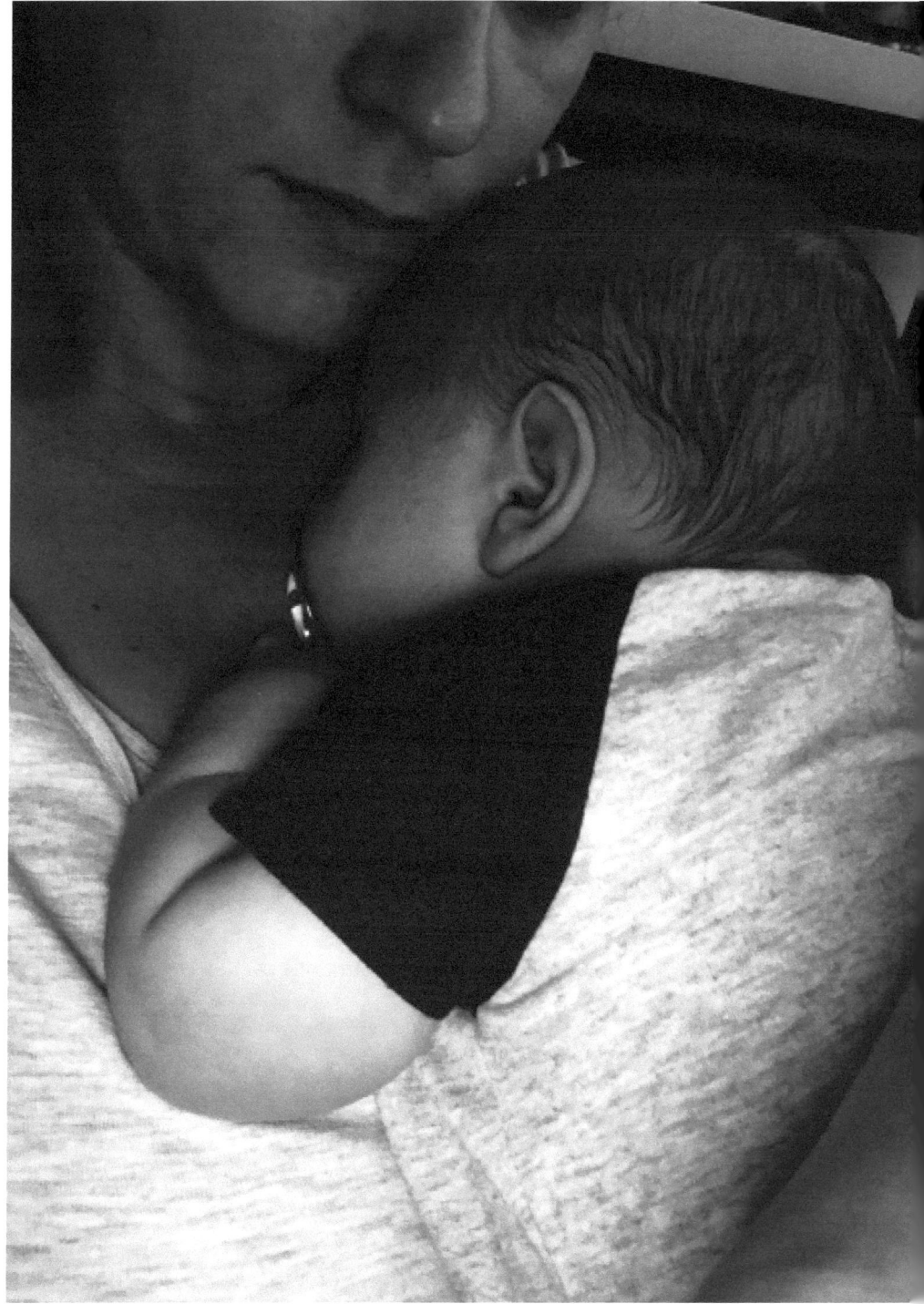

These are the thoughts in my head.

When asked about Motherhood, I always claim it to be the most difficult yet most rewarding thing I've done.

It is hard, firstly because it's new. It involves major learning. But who better to learn life skills from than you- my innocent joyous children. You can make any situation a happy one. It is also hard, because for some, it comes with major sleep deprivation. Let's face it, mothers need sleep to function, so we can figure out what it is you need when you cry. Motherhood is hard because sometimes we have to be the fun-police, encourage good habits and just say no. We have to let you fail sometimes so that you learn- even though we so desperately want to help you. We are there when you are sad and cry- which breaks our hearts. We care for you during sickness- which is terrible to watch and exhausting. So yes, I stand by it, Motherhood is difficult.

On the other hand, it is truly rewarding. Firstly, because nothing can prepare you for your heart overflowing with love. You, my children, are so pure-you say what you think. You are so caring and kind to others. You are so full of happiness and in awe of the discoveries you make in the big world around you. Watching the interactions between you fill me with so much love. Motherhood is also rewarding because it is full of firsts. Your first roll, your first taste of food, your first words, your first steps. You start learning some independence. You learn how to write your name and ride a bike for the first time. Only now as a mother, I truly appreciate these special moments. So yes, I stand by it, Motherhood is rewarding.

Motherhood has taught me innumerable things.

I want you to know that I'm not perfect, but I try. I don't have enough patience, but I'm working on it. I may complain, but nothing makes me happier than you. I want us to be the best of friends, so that you come to me with all your needs and worries first.

I have learnt a lot about myself through the experience of motherhood. But what I have learnt to appreciate the most, is what an amazing woman my own mother is. Nanny used to tell me I would only truly understand this when I became a mother and now I will tell you the same. I hope I can be a fraction of the selfless, caring and generous mother she is.

Lastly, I leave you with my prayers. I pray for your health, your safety, that you are well guided and well mannered. I pray you continue to be the caring, kind and funny individuals you are. I pray you are learners, that you ask questions when things don't seem right and that you are always happy. Above all else I hope you always emit utmost love to those around you and always receive the love you deserve. I pray I can continue this learning experience and be a better mother to you each and every day through both the difficult and the rewarding.

I love you more than you know.

Love, Mum.

Letter & Photography by Tahira Peer

Liyana and Alaia

A Perfect Mum

The Perfect Mum:

The Perfect mum helps her children with their homework;

The Perfect mum cooks for and feeds her children;

The Perfect mum supports her children in school and madressah;

The Perfect mum loves to bake;

The Perfect mum takes her children on adventures;

The Perfect mum teaches her children good values and morals;

The Perfect mum loves warm cuddles and kisses;

The Perfect mum is creative and likes to paint and do arts and crafts.

The Perfect mum, is our mum.

Story & Artwork By Liyana & Alaia Saheb

To put a child to sleep

To be allowed to lay a child into his bed.

To feel his eyelashes brushing against my cheek. Softly tickling as he is resisting to fall asleep. My fingers cuddling his hair, the baby curls in his neck. And his small fingers mirroring my movements.

From thinking "Now you really must go to sleep!" to thinking I can sit here forever, just looking at him sleeping, without a care in the world.

When I finally am allowed to put him to bed (Both he and his sister really prefer being tucked in by their dad. He is also the one making them their breakfast and getting them to and from kindergarten, as he also works there) But once in a blue moon I am allowed to read their bedtime stories, sing a lullaby and tuck them in. "Mamma, vil du sove med meg?" ("Mommy, will you sleep beside me?")

To my dearest Lotta & Paul.

Story & Photography by Helen Haukedal

POGLED SKOZI OKNO

Ste že kdaj pogledali skozi okno globoko v noči, priisluhnili šepetu zvokov in krohotajočih se glasov, ki so prihajali naproti skozi samoto tišine? Temne hitre sence v odsevu oken in topel vonj po domači jabolčni piti vznemirijo vse čute in vas počasi odnesejo nazaj v pozabljen svet spominov...

Stojim sredi najinega majhnega stanovanja. Ravno dovolj prostora, da odložim škatlo zraven mačjega stranišča. Spet so ga našli na vrtu, našega mačkona! Prav odleglo mi je, da so ga prinesli.

Poskušala sem mu dopovedati, da ne morem dvigati škatel, ker me še vedno boli. Kar usedel se je za mizo in se obrnil stran, povsem zamoten s svojimi smešnimi videi preko spleta. Ozrem se v strop z bolečino v sebi. Nobenemu nisem izdala svoje skrivnosti, a ta utripa vse močneje in glasneje v srcu. 'Ubila si otroka.'

Oglasi se zvonec in pred vrati je moja draga prijateljica, vsa obsijana s to posebno lepoto in iskrečim veseljem. Nočem vedeti. Srce mi zastane. Poskušam privleči vso srečo na dan, pa mi moje srce ne dovoli. Tako ji želim povedati, pa globoko v sebi vem, da ne bo mogla douumeti. Njena naivnost ji prizanese. Ima tisto nekaj, česar jaz nimam. Postane mi slabo. Pohitim do stranišča, da bi bruhala. Obstanem ob oknu in strmim na ulico. Prižgali so luči. Ulijejo se mi solze po obrazu in počutim se oropana življenja. Nato uzrem moškega skozi okno in njegov nasmeh je namenjen otroku. Vzame ga v svoje naročje in ga odnese v spalnico. Luči poniknejo v temi.

Minilo je deset let od takrat. Ležim na tleh in z roko sežem po telefonu. Glas na drugi strani slušalke mi prigovarja, naj se čimprej odpravim do urgence. 'Morala boš nadomestiti vso izgubljeno tekočino.' Komaj se vlečem čez mali hrib na poti do urgence, napor mi jemlje vso sapo. 'Ne smem izgibiti še tega otročka.' Strmim skozi okno bolnice. Povedali so mi, da je dojenček dobro in da lahko odidem domov. Kar naenkrat se usuje na tisoče lučk v temi in sijejo v noči kakor nešteto utrinkov sreče...

'Usedi se, draga moja. Na žalost je slaba novica.' Iz roke mi pade telefon in solze v trenutku prekrijejo obraz. 'A moje telo je še vedno noseče...pa bruhala sem še danes zjutraj...jaz...'

Obstanem na stolu in ure minejo. Zvok otroškega joka me predrami in zavem se, da se je zbudil. Objamem ga tesno in zašepetam 'Oprosti moj dragi sinek, ne morem ti pokloniti sestrice ali bratca...' Zibam svojega malega otročka nazaj v spanec in pogledam skozi okno v upanju, da zagledam to svetlo luč sijati na naju dva, želim verjeti, da vse bo zopet dobro. Morda pa ju zopet srečam v nebesih.

Looking through the window

Have you ever looked through the window at night, tuning into all those voices, laughs and whispers breaking through the silence of night? Dark shadows moving swiftly past the windows and warm apple pie smell coming through to greet you. And the memories take you away...

I'm back in our old tiny flat, barely enough room to put a box down next to the cat litter. They found him in the garden again! I'm so glad they brought the cat back. I tried to tell him I can't pick up the box because I'm still aching. He sat down and continued ignoring me, pulling out the chair and just started watching funny videos. I'm staring at the wall in pain. I've kept this quiet but in my head the voices are still getting louder by the minute. 'You've killed the baby.'

The door rings and my dearest friend comes in all chirpy and with that special glow. I didn't need to know. My heart sinks. I try and be happy for her but my heart won't let me. I wanted to tell her but I know she won't understand my pain. The blissful ignorance is kind to her. She's got something they've taken away from me. I feel sick. I'm running to the toilet to throw up. I stand next to the window and I catch myself staring down on the street. They've turned the street lamps on. My tears are running down my face and it feels like I've got no more life in me. But then I look at that man through the window and he's smiling down on his child. He carries the child to his bedroom and the lights go out.

It's been ten years since the last time and I'm lying on the floor reaching for the phone. The voice on the other side is urging me to go to the emergency. 'You need to get your fluids.' I'm almost passing out pushing myself up that little hill, gasping for air. 'I can't lose this baby. Not again.' I'm staring at the window in the hospital, they just told me the baby is doing well and I should be ok to go home. I'm watching the lights reflecting in the dark and it looks like a million sparkles exploding in happiness...

'I think you better sit down darling. I'm afraid it's bad news.' I dropped my phone and tears just covered my face without stopping. 'But my body is pregnant...I just vomited this morning...I...'

I just sit there in the dark and hours pass. The cry of the baby makes me realise he woke up. I hold him close and whisper 'I'm sorry baby but there will be no brother or sister...' As I'm rocking my baby back to sleep, I'm looking through that window again hoping to see a light to shine back on me and tell me that everything is going to be okay and I will meet them both in heaven one day.

Story written in Slovenian & English
Story & Photography by Tanja Fitisemanu

Legacy of an Adopted Child

Once there were two women who never knew each other, One - you do not remember, the other you call mother.

Two different lives shaped to make yours, One became your guiding star, the other became your sun.

The first gave you life, and the second taught you to live in it.

The first gave you a need for love and the second was there to give it.

One gave you a nationality; the other gave you a name.

One gave you the seed of talent; the other gave you an aim.

One gave you emotions; the other calmed your fears.

One saw your first sweet smile; the other dried your tears.

One gave you up - that's all she could do.

The other prayed for a child and God led her straight to you.

Now you ask through all your tears the age-old question through the years; Heredity or environment - which are you a product of?

Neither, my darling - neither - just two different kinds of love

* Author unknown
*at the time of print it is believed that the author of this poem wished to remain anonymous and has waived any copyright

First I was Jessica Perlas, but on a beautiful day in 1988 I became Jessica Svendsen. My mum and dad came all the way to the Philippines and brought me home to Norway. Today I'm 31 years old and I have an amazing family of my own.

When I was around 10 years old my mother gave me a diary. She wrote me a poem but I didn't understood the meaning of it. I still remember the look on her face when she wrote it. Her eyes were filled with joy, happiness and so much love. So maybe she was a bit disappointed when I didn't care as much as she had hoped I would.

The years went by and when I became a mother to a little baby boy, I finally understood. I understood how much every single word meant and what they still mean today.

Legacy of an adopted child is incredibly special to me because it amplified the bond between me and my mother and our relationship grows stronger and stronger each day.

My dear beautiful mother, there are no words for how thankful I am for being yours.

Story & Photography Jessica Parles Svendsen

Being a mother

Don't regret the times you could have spent with your mother or being a mother to your children.

Growing up in a family of eight children, with two mothers, made it hard to get attention from anyone unless you had done something wrong. Nevertheless my mothers' imparted lots of their knowledge and wisdom.

I learned to sew, crochet, bake, cook and tell stories from my biological mother. We would look at patterns and discuss them and find the easiest quickest way to make something simple into the most beautiful garment ever. She had such a wonderful imagination, could see what could be done before even starting and told us lots of stories about the fairies that live under the jacaranda tree in our front yard and how she knew they were there.

My step mother showed us that we all didn't need to be housewives in a time when very few women went out to work she went out to earn a little bit more for our household. So my mothers' had different talents. One was into arts, crafts and the homemaker, the other was the administrator and confident about her abilities to provide an extra income. Both had many friends so in addition to the many blood relatives we had many aunties and uncles who we visited often. Every one of these people contributed to the person I am today and gave me something I can pass on to my children and grandchildren.

For my sons: love, support and respect, unconditionally, the mother of your children in better ways than your mother was treated.

For my daughters: love yourselves enough so that you never settle for anything less than unconditional love, support and respect.

Story & Photography Shamina Khanum

Your Wonderful

A thousand small miracles manifest themselves
In the curl of your toes,
The thoughtfulness in your eyes
And the way your hair stands to attention.
Your wonderful is not lost on me.

I lay awake at night counting your breaths
In case they should stop.
Worrying if they are too short or too few.
Your lips suddenly curl and
Your shoulders lift in a silent reassuring giggle.
Your wonderful is not lost on me.

Three souls who might have become your friends
left this world before were able to know them.
I held you close and cried.
And I count my blessings every day.
Your wonderful is not lost on me.

When you snuggle up beside me
Because sleep does not come easy,
I remember the nights when I fell asleep
To the sounds of my mother's breath and
Your wonderful is not lost on me.

Even in my darkest moments.
When you're screaming, inconsolable,
Tired but unwilling to sleep.
As your little body wriggles in my arms and
I ask you over and over again, "what do you want?"
Your wonderful is not lost on me.

When I feel like I am failing you,
Tired and unable to keep up with your energy,
My soul aching from the way your
Midnight cries still echo in my mind.
Your wonderful is not lost on me.

Nestled in someone else's arms,
Your eyes still firmly fixed in my direction,
As if nothing else exists in this world
Your wonderful is not lost on me.

Of all the souls that have come my way,
It is yours that surprises me most.
I am daunted by your perfection and
Overwhelmed by your loveliness.
Your wonderful is not lost on me

A thousand small miracles manifest themselves
As time rushes by and
Somehow you grew from butterflies in my tummy
To a little boy who knows his own mind.
Your wonderful is not lost on me.

Poem & Photography By Ameera Karimshah

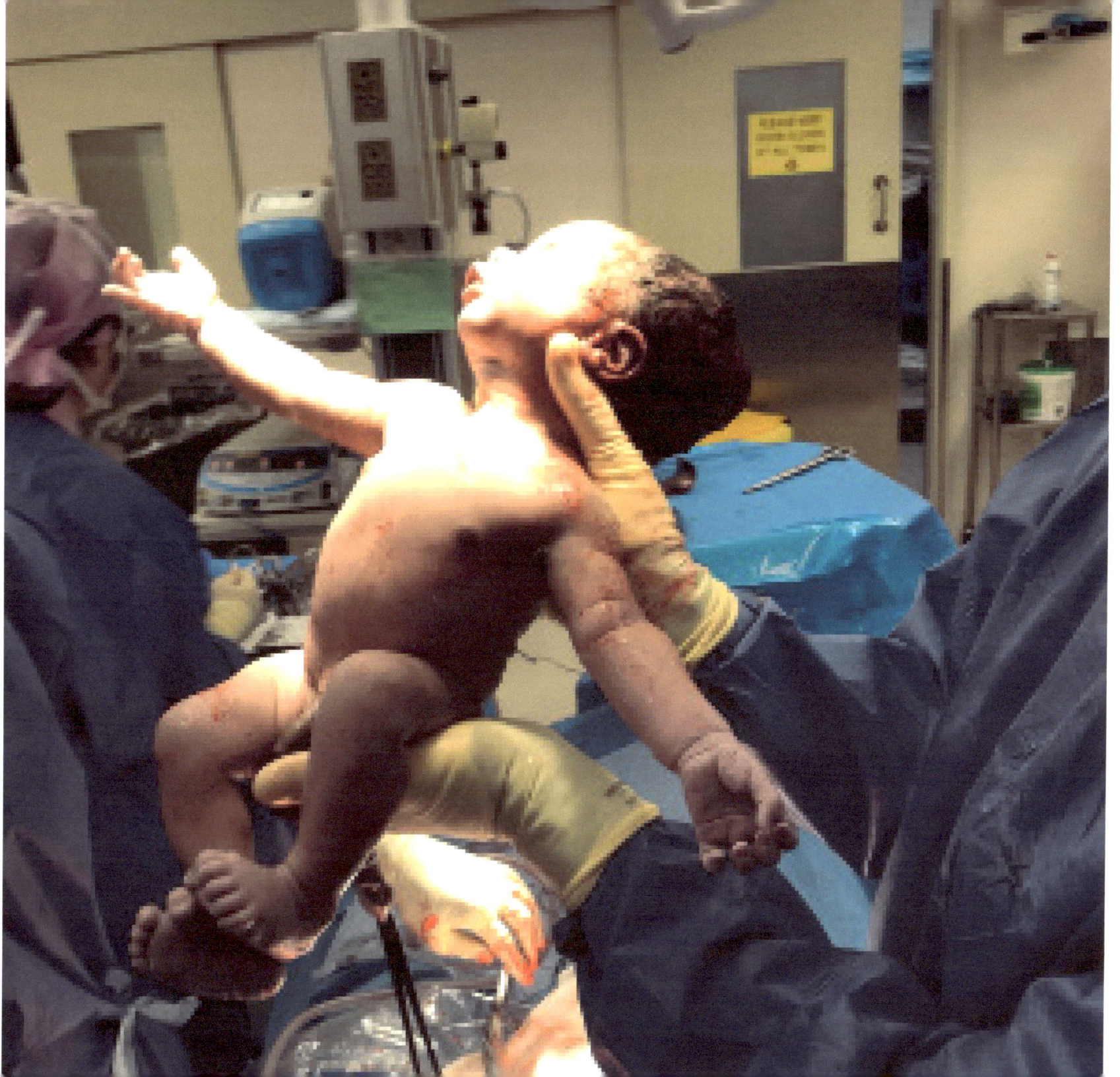

Respectful values

Ar dae member me mama en watin e learn me way ar bin small. Me Mama na bin fine woman en e bin get good heart for all man.

Way ar bin small me Mama learn me boku tin about motar man life, how for behave to other people dem na dis world e say because life na lek coin /paper way dae na book way dae flip over any tame to dae other side.

Me Mama tell me for treat everybody dae same because we all na one, weather you be poor or rich man, na God creat we all, en we nor know watin tumara dae bring.

Me Mama learn me for respect all man weather den young or den old e say because way you respect other people den, den go respect you sef, na dat ar apply na me life en e dae wok for me day leke tiday.

En e learn me for always be truthful even though people nor go lek am en e go help me for go on wit me life. Ar tell me Mama tenki for learn me all den good tin dem na dem dae help me na life tiday.

Lee e soul forever rest na perfect peace Amen.

Reflecting on my mother and what she taught me as a child. My mother was a beautiful woman with a heart of gold.

As a child my mother taught me things about life how to act and behave to other people in this world because life is like a coin/page in the pool that can flip at any time to the other side. She told me to treat everyone equal because we are all one, be it rich or poor all created by God and we never know what the future will bring in life.

She taught me how to respect people be it old or young because when you to, then you will receive it from them as well, which I applied in my life and it's working for me today.

I was taught to be truthful always even though people will not like it but it will help me to keep my head above the water.

I thank my mother for instilling me with these values. It elps me in my day-to-day life.

May her gentle soul forever rest in perfect peace Amen.

Story written in Pidgin & English
Story & Photography By Juliet Greene

Biographies

Ameera Karimshah

Ameera is the current Principal Executive Officer of 1000 Tales Co-op LTD. She is also the proud mama of 4 month old Taarun - her greatest teacher. Her daily prayer is that he grows up understanding his privilege and uses it to empower others.

Anna Vassadis

Anna Vassadis has a PhD in Sociology and has worked as a researcher on a wide range of projects for a number of years. In particular, her research interests include ethnicity, ethnic identity and culture, multiculturalism, and migration. Anna is also a keen writer, so when presented with the opportunity to write about her new experience as a mother she couldn't resist

Gayathiri Ganthithasan

Gayathiri Ganthithasan came to Australia 11 years ago, after living in Sri Lanka and completing her undergraduate studies in India. She is a mother to a 10 year old son and a two year old daughter. Gayathiri has a keen interest in Tamil literature and poetry.

Gurlovleen Kaur Sehmbi

I am Gurlovleen Kaur Sehmbi born and brought up in northern state of India called Punjab. So Punjabi is my mother language. I am not much of a writer but I love to write my heart out when I feel like sharing . I started writing letters to my son (the only child) when he was born. I am doing this every year on his birthday and this is the first time (on his 5th bday) I have decided to publish it. So, inspiration of writing is mostly concentrated on the people I love or my own emotions and feelings. Besides writing, I love to read, listen to the music and make handicrafts which is also mostly for myself or near ones. Professionally, I am web developer who loves to create websites.

Hayley Dry

Since my childhood, I have daydreamed about being an author. I have studied creative writing, linguistics, Indigenous Australian voices in literature and wondered how to get a good job in a remote Western Australian publishing house. Serendipitously, I ended up becoming a social worker, basing my profession in a specialist organisation supporting young refugee survivors of torture and trauma. I live with my Sri Lankan husband in a rambling Queenslander with four delightful ex-battery hens and a darling retired horse called Art (the love of my life). My husband and I are expecting our rainbow baby in August. We are building our life between Australia and Sri Lanka, under the palm trees.

Helén Haukedal

I live in beautiful Bergen in Norway, in a house filled with yarn, plants, books and instruments. We are four people living in our house: me (a teacher), my husband Daniel (a kindergarten teacher), and our cool children Lotta (5 years) and Paul (3 years). Trying to live in the moment, but I will always be a dreamer. My Instagram @porshelen

Jessica Edwards

Sunshin coast artist, Jessica Edwards, Paints usinf mixed media. Marrying acrylic paint, collage and soft pastels, she creates colourful and femimine inages on large canvas. If you have any questions about her artwork, she can be found at fyahflyart@ gmail.com. You can also find FyahFlyArt on instragrams and Facebook

Jessica Parles Svendsen

I live in the beautiful Hardanger fjord in Norway. Family is incredibly important to me and I enjoy every day I get to spend together with them. I have three beautiful children, Kevin, Emmy and Adelheid, and I have a partner, Kristian. They are a source of love and happiness to me and to everyone around them. My "missing piece", is the Philippines. So I hope one day I can travel to the Philippines and find all the missing pieces and share them with my family and friends.

Juliet Green

My name is Juliet F Greene. I am from Sierra Leone in West Africa originally, and now reside in Australia. I can here as a refugee from Ghana in 2004, now an Australian citizen. I am married with three lovely and beautiful children

Biographies

Lajla Darvill

My name is Lajla and I am originally from Croatia but have been calling Australia my home for the last 7 years. I am a mother of two, a beautiful and caring 4 year old girl and a cheeky and affectionate 10 month old boy. My children are my happiness and the reason I try to better myself every day.

Nazrana Shabeb

Nazrana is aged 33 - full time working mum of two amazing girls (Liyana and Alaia). Nothing gives me more pleasure than being a mum, and helping my girls grow to be strong, brave and independent.

Liyana Shabeb

Liyana 9 years old - enjoys singing and is a member of her school choir. She wants to be a teacher when she grows up, and is teaching herself how to illustrate characters for her short stories. Liyana is learning to speak Vietnamese and Arabic.

Alaia Shabeb

Alaia is 6 years old - enjoys dancing and singing and is a member of her school choir. She wants to be a police woman when she grows up and wants to start guitar lessons. Alaia is learning to speak Vietnamese and Arabic.

Nazmeera O'Reilly

Mother of two incredible little girls Imaani (5) and Aleena (6months). I work in the financial industry, currently on maternity leave with our newest addition to the family. I'm an avid reader, and enjoy spending time reading to my girls in hope they will one day have the same love for books that I do.

Imaani O'Reilly

Imaani is 5 years old and loves to colour dance and sing... and everything pink. She would like to be an Ice Cream Lady when she grows older.

Shamina Khanum

I was born into a large unconventional family in Harare, Zimbabwe. My father had two wives, so I had two mothers and seven siblings. I am currently studying complimentary medicine and healing practices which has always been an interest of mine. When I have time, I like to read, do some crafts and take walks on the beach. My greatest love is my children and in recent years my grandchildren.

Sharon Govender

Sharon is a new mother, having had her first child Kinnera in May 2017. She is currently on maternity leave and transitioning her little one into a family daycare whilst preparing to return to work.

Tahira Peer

My name is Tahira and I am from Brisbane, Australia. I have a wonderful husband and we have a 4 year old daughter and a 2 year old son who keep us very busy and entertained. My children understand my job title of Radiation Therapist to be working in a hospital and looking after sick people. My am passionate about my family and friends and spending time with them is what gives me joy.

Tanja Fitisemanu

Crafty Mama Network was born in late October 2017, created on a voluntary basis with intention to make a warm and beautiful space for creative moms and their businesses, hobbies and passions, supporting each other in any way we can. As a founder and mom of two, my main passion was to help growing, developing and helping expand our fellow Crafty Mama's dreams. We have created a Facebook group, Facebook page, Instagram account and are developing a website at this present time. Mama world is not an island but a whole wide world connected as a big family.

www.ingramcontent.com/pod-product-compliance
Lightning Source LLC
Chambersburg PA
CBHW042106090426

42811CB00018B/1867